Japanese Kanji For Beginners

Dr. Asuka Tsuchiya

CW01646100

Japanese Kanji for Beginners

ISBN: 978-1-914249-11-2

Published by Ameno Publishing

Copyright © 2021 Asuka Tsuchiya

Illustration by 小咲さと (Kosaki Sato)

Ancient Kanji Font 春秋 tsu by Tsumie Kaneko

The moral right of this author has been asserted.

All rights reserved. No part of this publication may be reproduced, stored in a retrieval system, or transmitted in any form or by any means without prior permission in writing from the publisher.

The publisher is not responsible for websites (or their content) not owned by the publisher.

www.funjapaneselearning.com

YouTube: Fun Japanese Learning

https://www.youtube.com/c/FunJapaneseLearning

Podcast: Fun Japanese Listening

Facebook: @Dr.AsukaTsuchiya

Instagram: @asuka.sensei

Introduction

After you've mastered all the Hiragana and Katakana letters,

You feel like…

"Now is the time to learn Kanji!"

But you are also wondering,

"How do I start?"

It's challenging to learn Kanji.

Kanji is VERY different from Hiragana and Katakana.

Hiragana and Katakana are phonetic letters. If you connect each letter and sound, you can pronounce it accurately (there are some exceptions, but you've already learnt them (^_^))

But each Kanji character has several readings.

"Oh, no, but Why!?" you may ask.

The origin of Kanji

Kanji came from China.

In the Chinese language, most Chinese characters have one reading. So even though the Chinese language has millions of Chinese characters, you can read it if you memorize each character's reading.

Then why do Japanese Kanji have several readings?

A long time ago, Japanese people imported the Chinese language and characters. At that time, we had the old Japanese language but didn't have writing systems. So we used the Chinese language to write.

Our ancestors soon noticed that Chinese characters represent meanings, and they also had Japanese words that shared similar meanings.

So they started using Chinese characters to represent Japanese words.

For example, the Chinese character 山 means mountain, and in the Chinese language, it's pronounced as "shān." Ancient Japanese people imported this sound as "サン." But the Japanese language also has the word "やま," which means mountain. So our ancestors attached the reading "やま" to the same kanji character 山.

As a result, the Kanji character 山 has two readings, サン, and やま.

Most Kanji characters have Chinese origin reading and Japanese origin reading.

Chinese origin reading is called On （おん） reading, for example, サン for 山. On the Kanji charts in this book, On reading is written in Katakana. It's a standard way of writing in the Japanese Kanji dictionary.

Japanese origin reading is called Kun（くん） reading, for example, やま for 山. Kun reading is written in Hiragana.

Also, Japanese people invented the original Japanese Kanji, which was developed and used in Japan only.

The origin of Kanji characters is the Chinese language, but it has been developed and Japanized in Japan.

How do Japanese people learn Kanji?

Many Kanji learners focus on memorizing On and Kun readings in the same way as remembering each Hiragana and Katakana letter reading.

But this way doesn't work well.

The same Kanji characters are pronounced differently in different words.

For example, Mt. Fuji is 富士山（ふ・じ・さん）, so the character 山 is pronounced as サン.

However, "I climb a mountain." is 山に　のぼります. The character 山 is pronounced as やま.

You need to memorize how to pronounce each Kanji word.

It is also helpful to build up your vocabulary.

You'll soon be getting familiar with Kanji words and confidently using them.

With this book, you'll learn 140 Kanji characters and related Kanji words.

It covers JLPT N5 level Kanji characters, which is perfect for beginners.

Let's start your Kanji learning journey with this book!

Asuka Sensei

How to use this book

Characters

おおいけせんせい
大池 先生

ふくたろう

るうこ

You learn Kanji with your teacher, おおいけ　せんせい, and two kids called ふくたろう and るうこ.

ふくたろう and るうこ are learning Kanji with you from おおいけせんせい.

What each section contains

Kanji characters at a glance

At the beginning of each chapter, you can glance at the Kanji characters and their basic meanings.

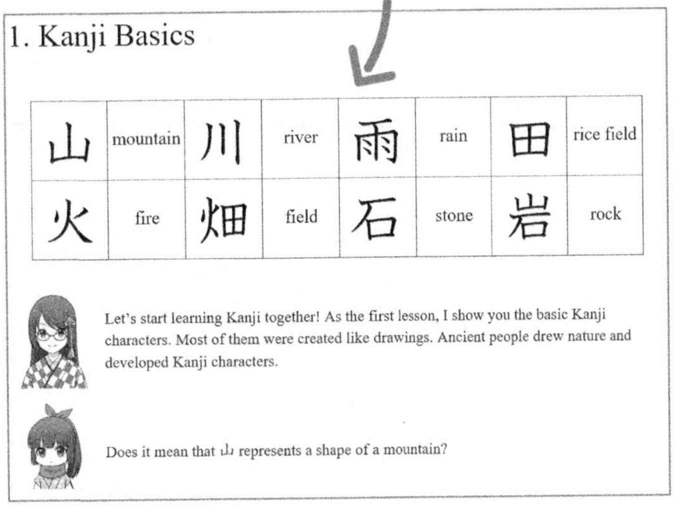

1. Kanji Basics

山	mountain	川	river	雨	rain	田	rice field
火	fire	畑	field	石	stone	岩	rock

Let's start learning Kanji together! As the first lesson, I show you the basic Kanji characters. Most of them were created like drawings. Ancient people drew nature and developed Kanji characters.

Does it mean that 山 represents a shape of a mountain?

Below the chart, おおいけせんせい、ふくたろう and るうこ have a chat related to the Kanji characters you will learn in each chapter.

Kanji Writing Practice

You can see Kanji characters with stroke order. The number shows the starting point of each line.

You can also check the meaning, On reading, Kun reading, and the related words.

On reading is written in Katakana, and Kun reading is written in Hiragana. The mark "・" separates each reading. If Kun reading requires Hiragana, it's written after "-." For example, ひと-つ means 一つ.

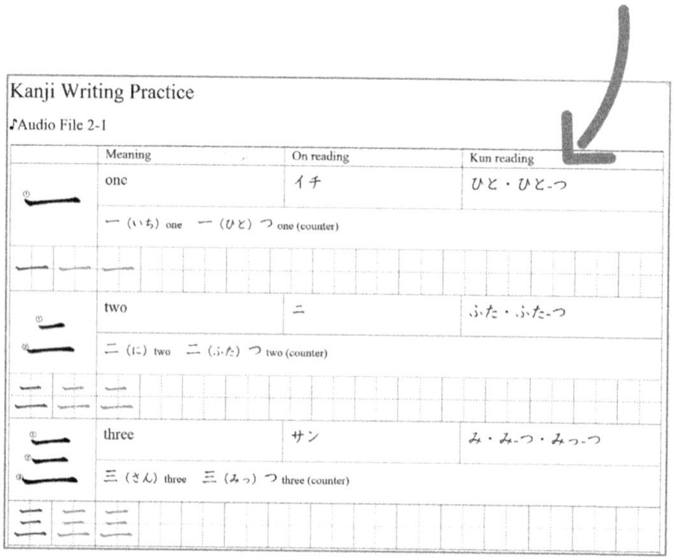

Kanji Writing Practice

♪Audio File 2-1

	Meaning	On reading	Kun reading
一	one	イチ	ひと・ひと-つ
	一（いち）one　一（ひと）つ one (counter)		
二	two	ニ	ふた・ふた-つ
	二（に）two　二（ふた）つ two (counter)		
三	three	サン	み・み-つ・みっ-つ
	三（さん）three　三（みっ）つ three (counter)		

Not sure how to pronounce each word? No worries. You can listen to the audio! Claim the free gift, the audio tracks to accelerate your Kanji learning. You can find how to download it in the next section.

*The readings shown in this book are based on the "Joyo Kanji list," the official list of Kanji characters in common use.

*The underline is added to a special reading for a particular word.

Reading Exercises

You can practice how to read each Kanji word and sentence with audio.

The answer section is at the end of this book.

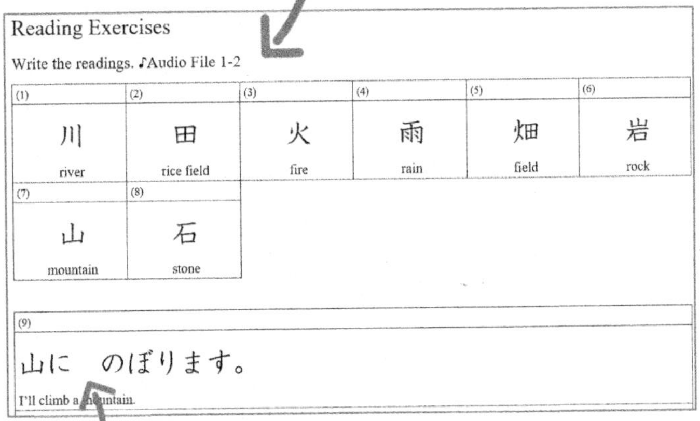
Reading Exercises

Write the readings. ♪Audio File 1-2

(1)	(2)	(3)	(4)	(5)	(6)
川 river	田 rice field	火 fire	雨 rain	畑 field	岩 rock
(7)	(8)				
山 mountain	石 stone				

(9)

山に　のぼります。

I'll climb a mountain.

*To make sentences easier to read, a gap between phrases is used sometimes.

Writing Exercises

You can practice how to write each Kanji word and sentence.

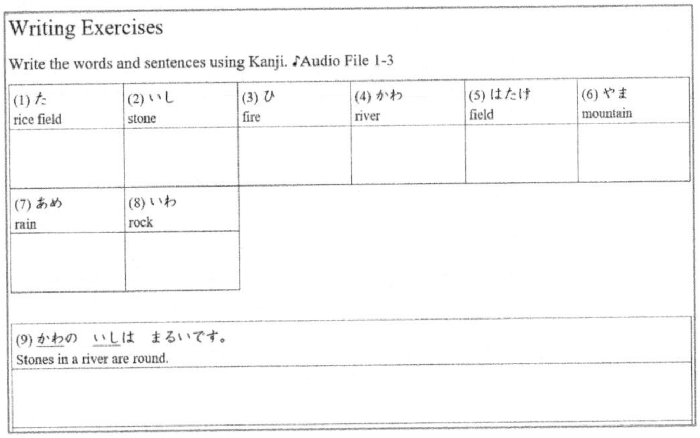
Writing Exercises

Write the words and sentences using Kanji. ♪Audio File 1-3

(1) た rice field	(2) いし stone	(3) ひ fire	(4) かわ river	(5) はたけ field	(6) やま mountain
(7) あめ rain	(8) いわ rock				

(9) かわの　いしは　まるいです。

Stones in a river are round.

*If you'd like, you can practice dictation exercises. Listen to the audio and write down each word and sentence. It helps to improve your listening and writing skills!

Review Exercises

After you finish all the chapters, you can try Review Exercises. This section is similar to the JLPT N5 Kanji section style. It would be an excellent preparation practice for you if you would like to pass JLPT N5!

How to download the bonus audio

The audio files for this book are available to download for free at

www.funjapaneselearning.com

You can find the link in the menu bar as "Bonus Download." Simply select this book title and follow the instructions to get the audio.

We recommend downloading the files directly to your computer, not to your tablet or phone, and extracting them there before adding them to your media library.

You can then put them on your tablet, phone, or any device you'd like to use.

On the download page, there is an instruction.

For Free Japanese Study Tips, Check out:

www.funjapaneselearning.com

Follow me!

YouTube: Fun Japanese Learning

https://www.youtube.com/c/FunJapaneseLearning

Facebook: @Dr.AsukaTsuchiya

Instagram: @asuka.sensei

Table of Contents

1. Kanji Basics

山	mountain	川	river	雨	rain	田	rice field
火	fire	畑	field	石	stone	岩	rock

Let's start learning Kanji together! As the first lesson, I show you the basic Kanji characters. Most of them were created like drawings. Ancient people drew nature and developed Kanji characters.

Does it mean that 山 represents a shape of a mountain?

That's right! In the old days, it was written like 

Wow!

The river was , and it becomes the current Kanji character 川.

It is the same as "rain"  雨, and "fire,"  火.

This type of Kanji characters is called 象形文字（しょうけいもじ）, which means represent the shape of the object.

Amazing! Do all Kanji characters represent the shape of nature?

No, not all of them. Ancient people developed another type of Kanji characters, which combine the shapes and show the meaning.

For example, the kanji character 田 now means “rice field,” but originally 田 meant any crop field. But in Japan, there are two types of crop fields. The rice field is filled with water, and the usual crop field is dry. So ancient Japanese people combined 火 (fire) and 田 together and created 畑 to represent the non-rice field. At that time, they fired the ground and made a field to raise crops.

That’s interesting.

岩(rock) is a similar example. The ancient people combined the character for stone, 石 and the character for mountain, 山, and made a new character for “rock,” 岩.

This type of Kanji is called 会意文字（かいいもじ）, which combined several Kanji characters and meanings to create a new character.

Kanji characters are really fascinating!

Kanji Writing Practice

♪Audio File 1-1

	Meaning	On reading	Kun reading
山	mountain	サン	やま
	山（やま）mountain		
川	river	セン	かわ
	川（かわ）river		
雨	rain	ウ	あめ・あま
	雨（あめ）rain		
田	rice field	デン	た
	田（た）・田（た）んぼ rice field　水田（すいでん）paddy field		
火	fire	カ	ひ・ほ
	火（ひ）fire		
畑	field		はた・はたけ
	畑（はたけ）crop field		

	Meaning	On reading	Kun reading
石	stone	セキ・シャク・コク	いし
	石（いし）stone　石（せっ）けん soap		
岩	rock	ガン	いわ
	岩（いわ）rock		

石石石石石石石石石石石石石石石

岩岩岩

Reading Exercises

Write the readings. ♪Audio File 1-2

(1)	(2)	(3)	(4)	(5)	(6)
川 river	田んぼ rice field	火 fire	雨 rain	畑 crop field	岩 rock

(7)	(8)
山 mountain	石 stone

(9)

山に　のぼります。

I'll climb a mountain.

(10)

石けんで　あらいます。

I wash with a bar of soap.

(11)

雨です。

`It is rainy.

Writing Exercises

Write the words and sentences using Kanji. ♪Audio File 1-3

(1) た rice field	(2) いし stone	(3) ひ fire	(4) かわ river	(5) はたけ crop field	(6) やま mountain

(7) あめ rain	(8) いわ rock

(9) かわの　いしは　まるいです。 Stones in a river are round.
(10) あそこに　おおきい　いわが　あります。 There is a big rock over there.
(11) やまかわさんが　はたけに　います。 Ms. Yamakawa is in a crop field.

Ten types of Kanji strokes

There are ten essential types of Kanji strokes. If you understand each stroke line, you can write Kanji characters more easily.

1. Horizontal line

石	一	二	雨	田

2. Vertical line

山	川	水	十	木

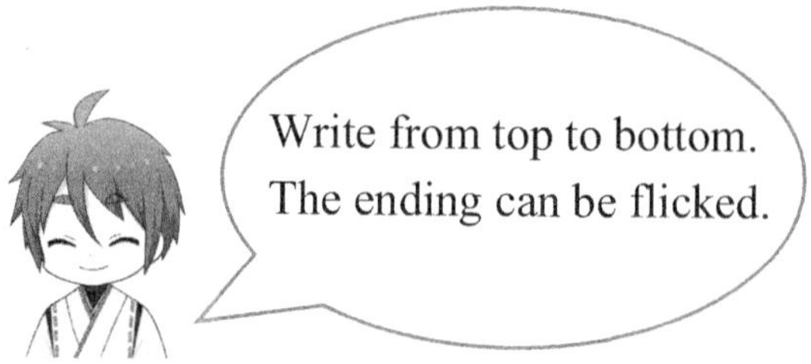

3. Slanting line

火	石	岩	木	人

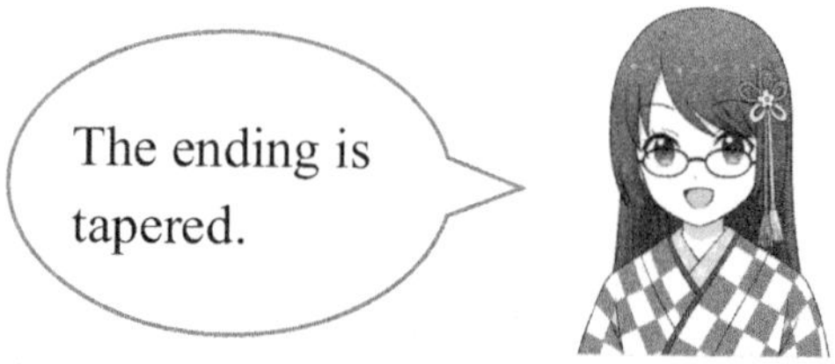

4. Right angle

田	雨	石	山	日

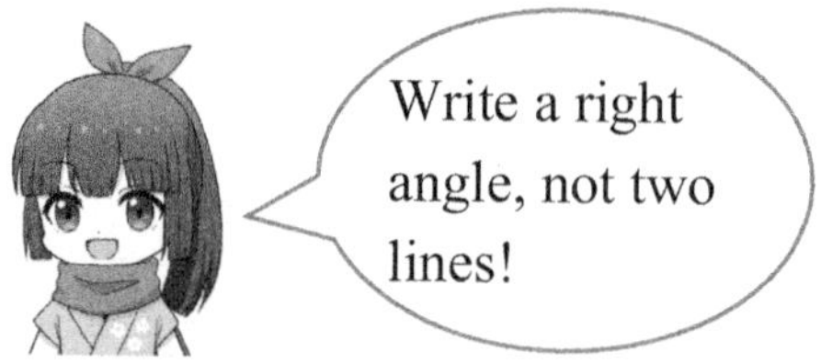

5. Slanting hook

水	力	夕	子	空

6. Curving hook

手	子	字	学	好

7. Fish hook

先	見	花	元	電

8. く shape

女	母

9. Duck shape

九	気

10. Dot

雨	火	父	母	魚

2. Numbers

一	one	二	two	三	three	四	four
五	five	六	six	七	seven	八	eight
九	nine	十	ten				

Now we learn Kanji characters for numbers.

Look at the character, "一," which means number one.

Oh, it's easy! One horizontal line!

Yes. Use one horizontal line to represent number one.

Number one has no shape, but if you use a line, you can show the **concept** of number one.

This type of Kanji characters is called 指示文字（しじもじ）. 指示文字 visualizes the concept.

So one 一, two 二, three 三… Oh, from number 4, they look different.

Yes. From number four, ancient people used other ways to represent numbers.

For example, the Kanji character for a number four 四 represents a mouth that exhales the air to show the pronunciation, "シ," as it's the same pronunciation as the number four.

It's interesting but not so helpful to memorize a character.

No. Learning the origin of Kanji often makes it easier to memorize, but not always.

How can we use these Kanji characters?

When you use them as pure mathematical numbers, we read them as 一（いち）二（に）三（さん）四（し/よん）五（ご）六（ろく）七（なな/しち）八（はち）九（く/きゅう）十（じゅう）.

Number four, seven, and nine have two names.

Yes. Each word chooses which number name. For example, nine o'clock is 九時（くじ）and nine minutes is 九分（きゅうふん）.

Oh, no. It's so complicated….

That's why it's important to memorize each word and its pronunciation!

Oh, I see.

When we count objects, we don't use pure numbers but "counters." Counters show both the quantity and quality of the things. We have many types of counters.

Here is a general counter to count objects. 一（ひと）つ、二（ふた）つ、三（みっ）つ、四（よっ）つ、五（いつ）つ、六（むっ）つ、七（なな）つ、八（やっ）つ、九（ここの）つ、十（とお）.

Oh, we read the Kanji character 十 as "じゅう" when we use it as a pure number and as "とお" when we use it as a counter.

Yes. To read Kanji correctly, you need to think about how it's used in a context.

Kanji Writing Practice

♪Audio File 2-1

	Meaning	On reading	Kun reading
一	one	イチ・イツ	ひと・ひと-つ
	一（いち）one　一（ひと）つ one (counter)		
一 一 一			
二	two	ニ	ふた・ふた-つ
	二（に）two　二（ふた）つ two (counter)		
二 二 二			
三	three	サン	み・み-つ・みっ-つ
	三（さん）three　三（みっ）つ three (counter)		
三 三 三			
四	four	シ	よ・よ-つ・よっ-つ・よん
	四（し / よん）four　四（よっ）つ four (counter)		
四 四 四			
五	five	ゴ	いつ・いつ-つ
	五（ご）five　五（いつ）つ five (counter)		
五 五 五			
六	six	ロク	む・む-つ・むっ-つ・むい
	六（ろく）six　六（むっ）つ six (counter)		
六 六 六			

	Meaning	On reading	Kun reading
七	seven	シチ	なな・なな-つ・なの
	七（しち / なな）seven　七（なな）つ seven (counter)		
七 七 七			
八	eight	ハチ	や・や-つ・やっ-つ・よう
	八（はち）eight　八（やっ）つ eight (counter)		
八 八 八			
九	nine	キュウ・ク	ここの・ここの-つ
	九（きゅう / く）nine　九（ここの）つ nine (counter)		
九 九 九			
十	ten	ジュウ・ジッ	とお・と
	十（じゅう）ten　十（とお）ten (counter)		
十 十 十			

Reading Exercises

Write the readings. ♪Audio File 2-2

(1)	(2)	(3)	(4)	(5)	(6)
二 two	四 four	六 six	九 nine	一 one	八 eight
(7)	(8)	(9)	(10)	(11)	(12)
三 three	十 ten	五 five	七 seven	二つ two (counter)	五つ five (counter)
(13)	(14)	(15)	(16)		
八つ eight (counter)	四つ four (counter)	九つ nine (counter)	六つ six (counter)		

(17)
ハンバーガーを　三つください。 Please give me three hamburgers.
(18)
テーブルのうえに　みかんが七つあります。 There are seven tangerine oranges on a table.
(19)
たまごが　一つもありません。 There is no egg.

Writing Exercises

Write the words and sentences using Kanji. ♪Audio File 2-3

(1) ひとつ one (counter)	(2) よっつ four (counter)	(3) みっつ three (counter)	(4) とお ten (counter)	(5) むっつ six (counter)	(6) ここのつ nine (counter)
(7) ななつ seven (counter)	(8) し four	(9) に two	(10) じゅう ten	(11) ご five	(12) さん three
(13) はち eight	(14) ろく six	(15) いち one	(16) なな seven	(17) く nine	

(18) カレーライスを　ふたつ　ください。 Please give me two curries and rice.
(19) けしゴムを　いつつ　かいました。 I bought five erasers.
(20) りんごが　やっつ　あります。 There are eight apples.

3. Family

父	father	母	mother	子	child	人	people
男	man	女	woman	友	friend	犬	dog

Now we learn Kanji characters for a family!

Father, Mother, child… How can we call “boy” in Japanese?

Good question! A boy is 男（おとこ）の子（こ）, male child. And a girl is 女（おんな）の子（こ）, female child. 男 （おとこ）means man and 女 （おんな）means woman but we usually call men as 男（おとこ）の人（ひと）, male person, and women as 女（おんな）の人（ひと）, female person.

Male child, 男（おとこ）の子（こ） becomes male person 男（おとこ）の人（ひと）, when he grows up.

That’s easy to remember! How about mother and father?

When we call our father directory, or when we refer someone's father, we use "お父（とう）さん," but when we refer our father to someone else, we call him "父（ちち）."

Without お and さん!

Yes. When we mention our family member to someone, we omit any honorifics.

Is it the same as our mother? When we call her directory or when we refer someone's mother, "お母（かあ）さん" is used, but when we mention our own mother to someone else, "母（はは）" is used?

Yes, that's right!

お母（かあ）さん and 母（はは）sound very different, but if you see a kanji character, you can understand the meaning.

Kanji is really useful to guess the meaning!

I would like to tell you one more thing. 人 is used as a counter when we count people, such as 一人, 二人, 三人 but you need to be careful how to pronounce.

One person, 一人（ひとり）, and two people, 二人（ふたり）, have a unique reading.

More than three people, we count number and にん, such as, 三人（さんにん）, 四人（よにん）, 五人（ごにん）, 六人（ろくにん）, 七人（ななにん）or（しちにん）, 八人（はちにん）, 九人（きゅうにん）or（くにん）, and 十人（じゅうにん）.

It is interesting!

一人（ひとり） and 二人（ふたり） sound similar with 一（ひと）つ and 二（ふた）つ.

More than three people use usual numbers, such as 三（さん）, 四（よん）, 五（ご）etc.

That's right! Well done!

Kanji Writing Practice

♪Audio File 3-1

	Meaning	On reading	Kun reading
父	father	フ	ちち
	父（ちち）my father　お父（とう）さん father		
母	mother	ボ	はは
	母（はは）my mother　お母（かあ）さん mother		
子	child	シ・ス	こ
	子（こ）ども child		
人	people	ジン・ニン	ひと
	一人（ひとり）one people　二人（ふたり）two people　三人（さんにん）three people		
男	man	ダン・ナン	おとこ
	男（おとこ）の人（ひと）man　男（おとこ）の子（こ）boy		
女	woman	ジョ・ニョ・ニョウ	おんな
	女（おんな）の人（ひと）woman　女（おんな）の子（こ）girl		

	Meaning	On reading	Kun reading
友	friend	ユウ	とも
	友（とも）だち friend		
友 友 友 友			
犬	dog	ケン	いぬ
	犬（いぬ）dog		
犬 犬 犬 犬			

Reading Exercises

Write the readings. ♪Audio File 3-2

(1)	(2)	(3)	(4)	(5)	(6)
母 my mother	父 my father	子ども child	犬 dog	友だち friend	一人 one person
(7)	(8)	(9)	(10)	(11)	(12)
二人 two people	三人 three people	男の人 man	女の子 girl	お母さん mother	お父さん father

(13)
お母さんと子ども a mother and a child
(14)
男の子が三人います。 There are three boys.
(15)
女の人が二人と犬がいます。 There are two women and a dog.

Writing Exercise

Write the words and sentences using Kanji. ♪Audio File 3-3

(1) おとこのこ	(2) おんなのこ	(3) ちち	(4) はは	(5) ともだち	(6) こども
boy	girl	my father	my mother	friend	child
(7) おとうさん	(8) おかあさん	(9) おんなのひと	(10) ひとり	(11) ふたり	(12) さんにん
father	mother	woman	one person	two people	three people

(13) クラスに　おとこのこが　にじゅうにんと　おんなのこが　じゅうろくにん　います。 There are twenty boys and sixteen girls in a class.
(14) ははと　ちちは　げんきです。 My mother and my father are healthy.
(15) ともだちの　うちに　いぬが　います。 There is a dog in my friend's house.

4. Days of the Week

日	the Sun, day	曜	day of the week	月	the Moon, month	水	water
木	tree	金	gold, metal	土	ground		

Do you know what “Sunday” is called in Japanese?

Yes, of course! にちようび.

Well done! Then, do you know how we write にちようび using Kanji?

No, I don’t know.

We write it like this. “日曜日（にちようび）.”

Wow! The first and the last characters are the same, but they are read differently!

Yes. The first Kanji represents “the Sun.” The rest part, 曜日（ようび）shows “the day of the week.” The character 日 means “the Sun” and “day,” as one day is one Sun cycle, from sunrise to the next.

日曜日（にちようび）literally means Sunday!

Then, how about the other days of the week?

Monday is 月曜日（げつようび）. The first character means the Moon. 月曜日 is Moon day.

Tuesday is 火曜日（かようび）. 火 means fire. 火曜日 is Fire day.

Wednesday is 水曜日（すいようび）. 水 means water. 水曜日 is Water day.

Thursday is 木曜日（もくようび）. 木 means tree. 木曜日 is Tree day.

Friday is 金曜日（きんようび）. 金 means gold. 金曜日 is Gold day.

Saturday is 土曜日（どようび）. 土 means ground. 土曜日 is Ground day.

Wow. It’s interesting!

The character of the Moon 月 also means “month” because traditionally, Japanese people used the Lunar calendar and one Moon cycle is one month.

Wow. That makes sense!

We count each month of the year. For example, January is 一月（いちがつ）, February is 二月（にがつ）.

How about “one month”?

We call one month as “一（いっ）か月（げつ），” two months as 二（に）か月（げつ）, three months as “三（さん）か月（げつ）” and so on.

Oh, no. The same Kanji 月 is used but pronounced differently, “がつ” and “げつ”!

Kanji Writing Practice ♪Audio File 4-1

	Meaning	On reading	Kun reading
日	the Sun, day	ニチ・ジツ	ひ・か
	一日（いち・にち one day/ついたち the first day of the month） 二日（ふつか）two days, the second day of the month 十一日（じゅう・いち・にち）eleven days, the eleventh day of the month		
日 日 日			
曜	day of the week	ヨウ	
	日曜日（にち・よう・び）Sunday 火曜日（か・よう・び）Tuesday		
曜 曜 曜			
月	the Moon, month	ゲツ・ガツ	つき
	月曜日（げつ・よう・び）Monday 一月（いち・がつ）January 一（いっ）か月（げつ） one month 月（つき）the Moon		
月 月 月			
水	water	スイ	みず
	水曜日（すい・よう・び）Wednesday 水（みず）water		
水 水 水			
木	tree	ボク・モク	き・こ
	木曜日（もくようび）Thursday 木（き）tree		
木 木 木			
金	gold, metal	キン・コン	かね・かな
	金曜日（きんようび）Friday お金（かね）money		
金 金 金			

	Meaning	On reading	Kun reading
土	ground	ド・ト	つち
	土曜日（どようび）Saturday　土（つち）soil, ground		
土 土 土			

Reading Exercises

Write the readings. ♪Audio File 4-2

(1)	(2)	(3)	(4)	(5)	(6)
土 soil, ground	木 tree	月 Moon	お金 money	水 water	一日 one day
(7)	(8)	(9)	(10)	(11)	(12)
一日 the first day of the month	火曜日 Tuesday	木曜日 Thursday	月曜日 Monday	金曜日 Friday	日曜日 Sunday
(13)	(14)	(15)	(16)		
水曜日 Wednesday	土曜日 Saturday	三月 March	五か月 five months		

(17)

二月九日は土曜日です。

February the ninth is Saturday.

(18)

日曜日に　はたらきます。

I work on Sunday.

(19)

アメリカに十か月いました。

I stayed in the US for ten months.

Writing Exercise

Write the words and sentences using Kanji. ♪Audio File 4-3

(1) ふつか the second day of the month/ two days	(2) よっか the fourth day of the month/ four days	(3) むいか the sixth day of the month/ six days	(4) ようか the eighth day of the month/ eight days	(5) とおか the tenth day of the month/ ten days	(6) よんかげつ four months
(7) かようび Tuesday	(8) もくようび Thursday	(9) にちようび Sunday	(10) げつようび Monday	(11) すいようび Wednesday	(12) どようび Saturday
(13) きんようび Friday	(14) ろくがつ June	(15) じゅうがつ October	(16) しちがつ July	(17) つき Moon	(18) みず water

(19) しがつ　じゅうよっか April the fourteenth
(20) はちがつに　オーストラリアへ　いきます。 I'll go to Australia in August.
(21) おかねは　たいせつです。 Money is important.

The general rule of Kanji stroke order

It may be tricky to memorize Kanji stroke order. But actually, there are basic rules to follow.

If you know these general rules, you can write Kanji characters confidently!

1. From top to bottom

三

2. From left to right

川

3. Horizontal line comes first, and a vertical line comes second

十

4. Middle line comes first

水

5. Left slanting line comes first

人

6. Outside comes first

月

7. Crossing vertical line comes later

中

8, Crossing horizontal line comes later

子

5. Time 1

時	time	分	minute	半	half	前	before, front
後	after, back	午	(horse)	間	between, period	早	early

I know these Kanji characters for time expressions!

1:00 is 一時（いちじ）. 分 means minutes, and it is used like 五分（ごふん）.

Well done!

3:30 is 三時三十分（さんじさんじゅっぷん） or 三時半（さんじはん）.

半 means half.

Does the Kanji character 時 have two parts?

Yes!

The right side of 時 is 寺, and it represents the reading, ジ. This 寺 character has On reading ジ, and it means "temple." However, in 時 character, the meaning of the character 寺 is ignored, and only the On reading is used.

The left side of 時 is 日 the Sun. In ancient times, people told the time by the Sun's moving. So the left side 日 shows the meaning of this 時 character, "time."

This type of Kanji characters is called 形声文字（けいせいもじ）. Half part of Kanji shows the reading, and the other half shows the meaning. It is the most common type of Kanji.

Wow!

How do you say a.m. and p.m.?

Good question!

午前（ごぜん）is a.m. and 午後（ごご） is p.m.. We put them first.

For example, 2:00 p.m. is 午後（ごご）二時（にじ）.

I know that the character 前 means the front or before. But why does 午前（ごぜん） mean a.m.?

Good question! The character 午 means “horse.”

Have you ever heard about the 12 animals each year? Maybe you’ve seen them in Chinese New Year. It changes every year. For example, 2021 is the year of the cow.

Ah, yes. I’ve heard of that!

Traditionary, we also have the animal of the month, the animal of the day, and the animal of the time. The horse, 午, is the animal for noon, midday. So, 午前 means "before horse time." 午後 means "after horse time."

Wow, that's interesting! Then how to call 12:00 noon (midday)?

It is 正午（しょうご）. The character 正 means "just." So it means "just horse time." By the way, even though 午 means "horse," this character is now used only for the animal of the year or time and NOT used for the actual horse. The character for the real horse is 馬. You'll learn it later in this book.

I love horses. Glad to know we have two Kanji characters for them!

Kanji Writing Practice

♪Audio File 5-1

	Meaning	On reading	Kun reading
時	time	ジ	とき
	三時（さん・じ）three o'clock		
時 時 時			
分	minute, divide	ブン・フン・ブ	わ-ける・わ-かれる・わ-かる・わ-かつ
	一分（いっ・ぷん）one minute		
分 分 分			
半	half	ハン	なか-ば
	二時半（に・じ・はん）2:30　半分（はん・ぷん）half		
半 半 半			
前	before, front	ゼン	まえ
	前（まえ）before, front		
前 前 前			
後	back, after	ゴ・コウ	のち・うし-ろ・あと・おく-れる
	後（うし）ろ back, after		
後 後 後			
午	(horse)	ゴ	
	午前（ご・ぜん） morning, a.m.　午後（ご・ご） afternoon, p.m.		
午 午 午			

	Meaning	On reading	Kun reading
間	between	カン・ケン	あいだ・ま
	時間（じ・かん）time　一時間（いち・じ・かん）one hour		
間 間 間			
早	early	ソウ	はや-い・はや-まる・はや-める
	早（はや）い early		
早 早 早			

Reading Exercises

Write the readings. ♪Audio File 5-2

(1)	(2)	(3)	(4)	(5)	(6)
半分 half	後ろ back	前 front	午前 a.m.	午後 p.m.	時間 time
(7)	(8)	(9)	(10)	(11)	(12)
二時 2:00	四時半 4:30	三分 three minutes	五時 5:00	九分 nine minutes	七分 seven minutes
(13)	(14)	(15)	(16)	(17)	
九時 9:00	七時 7:00	四分 four minutes	十二時 12:00	早い early	

(18)

午前六時に　おきました。

I woke up at 6:00 am.

(19)

午後十一時に　ねました。

I went to bed at 11:00 pm.

(20)
ぎんこうの　前に　きっさてんが　あります。
There is a café in front of a bank.

Writing Exercise

Write the words and sentences using Kanji. ♪Audio File 5-3

(1) いちじ 1:00	(2) にじ 2:00	(3) さんじ 3:00	(4) よじ 4:00	(5) ごじはん 5:30	(6) ろくじ 6:00
(7) しちじ 7:00	(8) はちじ 8:00	(9) くじ 9:00	(10) じゅうじ 10:00	(11) じゅういちじ 11:00	(12) じゅうにじ 12:00
(13) にじはん 2:30	(14) ろっぷん six minutes	(15) ごぜん a.m.	(16) ごご p.m.	(17) じかん time	(18) はやい early

(19) レストランは　ごご　ごじからです。 The restaurant is open from 5:00 pm.
(20) じかんが　ありません。 I don’t have time.
(21) ろくじ　にじゅうごふんです。 It is 6:25.

6. Time 2

年	year	毎	every	週	week	今	now
朝	morning	昼	daytime	方	direction	夕	evening
夜	night						

Another group of time expressions!

The character, 毎, which means “every,” is really useful! 毎年（まいとし）is “every year,” 毎月（まいつき）is “every month,” 毎週（まいしゅう） is “every week,” 毎日（まいにち） is “every day”!

“Every morning” is 毎朝（まいあさ）.

Yes, well done!

The character 今 also looks useful.

That's right! “This year” is 今年（ことし）, “this month” is 今月（こんげつ）, “this week” is 今週（こんしゅう）.

But be careful! “Today” is 今日（きょう） and “this morning” is 今朝（けさ）.

These pronunciations are tricky, but when we see these words, 今日, and 今朝, it may be easier to guess the meaning.

Indeed! That's a significant part of kanji learning.

How do we say, for example, “last year” and “next week”?

Great question! We'll learn them later in this book!

I can't wait!

Kanji Writing Practice

♪Audio File 6-1

	Meaning	On reading	Kun reading
年	year	ネン	とし
	十年（じゅう・ねん）ten years		
年 年 年			
毎	every	マイ	
	毎年（まい・とし）every year　毎日（まい・にち）every day　毎月（まい・つき）every month		
毎 毎 毎			
週	week	シュウ	
	毎週（まい・しゅう）every week　一週間（いっ・しゅう・かん）one week		
週 週 週			
今	now	コン・キン	いま
	今日（きょう）today　今年（こ・とし）this year　今月（こん・げつ）this month 今週（こん・しゅう）this week		
今 今 今			
朝	morning	チョウ	あさ
	朝（あさ）morning　今朝（けさ）this morning　毎朝（まい・あさ）every morning		
朝 朝 朝			
昼	daytime	チュウ	ひる
	昼（ひる）day time　昼（ひる）ごはん lunch		
昼 昼 昼			

	Meaning	On reading	Kun reading
方	direction	ホウ	かた
	あの方（かた）that person (polite)		
夕	evening	セキ	ゆう
	夕方（ゆう・がた）evening　夕やけ（ゆう・やけ）sunset　夕日（ゆう・ひ）the setting sun		
夜	night	ヤ	よ・よる
	夜（よる）night		

Reading Exercises

Write the readings. ♪Audio File 6-2

(1)	(2)	(3)	(4)	(5)	(6)
昼 daytime	夜 night	夕方 evening	毎日 every day	毎年 every year	毎朝 every morning
(7)	(8)	(9)	(10)	(11)	(12)
今朝 this morning	今日 today	今週 this week	今月 this month	今年 this year	一週間 one week

(13)

今朝　朝ごはんを　たべましたか。

Did you eat breakfast this morning?

(14)

あの方は　どなたですか。

Who is that person?

(15)
夕やけが　きれいでした。 The sunset was beautiful.

Writing Exercises

Write the words and sentences using Kanji. ♪Audio File 6-3

(1) ごねん five years	(2) あさ morning	(3) ひる daytime	(4) ゆうがた evening	(5) よる night	(6) けさ this morning
(7) きょう today	(8) あのかた that person (polite)	(9) まいとし every year	(10) こんげつ this month	(11) まいにち every day	(12) ことし this year
(13) まいつき every month	(14) こんしゅう this week	(15) ゆうひ the setting sun	(16) まいしゅう every week	(17) まいあさ every morning	(18) いっしゅうかん one week

(19) さんねんまえ　フランスに　いきました。 I went to France three years ago.
(20) けさ　コーヒーを　のみました。 I had coffee this morning.
(21) じゅうにじに　ひるごはんを　たべませんか。 Shall we eat lunch at 12:00?

7. School

学	learn	校	school	先	ahead	生	live
本	book	語	narrate	英	UK, superior	名	name
字	letter, character	書	write	読	read	休	rest

Now here are the kanji characters related to school.

The character 学 means "learn," and 校 means "school." 学校（がっこう）is school.

I know 先生（せんせい）means "teacher," but why?

Good question! The character 先 means "ahead," and 生 means "live." Someone who lives ahead of us and leads us is a teacher.

Oh, I see.

先 is also used in time expression. 先月（せんげつ）means “last month” and 先週（せんしゅう）means “last week.”

I have a question. 本 is “book.” Why does 日本（にほん） mean “Japan?”

Great question!

The character 本 also means “source.” 日本 means “the source of the Sun.” From China, Japan is on the east side, and the Sun rises from Japan. That’s why ancient people called Japan the source of the Sun.

Interesting.

I have another question. The character 語 means “language,” and it’s used like 日本語（にほんご）, the Japanese language, or フランス語（ご）, the French language.

Why does 英語（えいご）means the English language?

Great question! A long time ago, our ancestors used Kanji to represent foreign words. Nowadays, the UK is written as イギリス in Katakana, but at that time, it was written as “英吉利（イギリス）” in Kanji. The first Kanji character, 英, and 語 were combined, and the word 英語（えいご）, the English language, was created.

It’s interesting! Kanji words contain the history of Japan, indeed!

Kanji Writing Practice

♪Audio File 7-1

	Meaning	On reading	Kun reading
学	learn	ガク	まな-ぶ
	学（まな）ぶ learn		
学 学 学			
校	school	コウ	
	学校（がっ・こう）school		
校 校 校			
先	ahead	セン	さき
	先月（せん・げつ）last month　先週（せん・しゅう）last week		
先 先 先			
生	live	セイ・ショウ	い-きる・い-かす・い-ける・う-まれる・う-む・お-う・は-える・は-やす・き・なま
	先生（せん・せい）teacher　学生（がく・せい）student		
生 生 生			
本	book	ホン	もと
	本（ほん）book　本（ほん）だな bookshelf　日本（に・ほん）Japan　日本人（に・ほん・じん）Japanese people		
本 本 本			

	Meaning	On reading	Kun reading
語	narrate	ゴ	かた-る・かた-らう
	日本語（に・ほん・ご）Japanese language		
語 語 語			
英	The United Kingdom, superior	エイ	
	英語（えい・ご）English language		
英 英 英			
名	name	メイ・ミョウ	な
	名前（な・まえ）name		
名 名 名			
字	letter, character	ジ	あざ
	字（じ）letter, character　名字（みょう・じ）family name		
字 字 字			
書	write	ショ	か-く
	字（じ）を書（か）く to write (letters/characters)		
書 書 書			
読	read	ドク・トク・トウ	よ-む
	本（ほん）を読（よ）む to read a book		
読 読 読			

休	rest	キュウ	やす-む・やす-まる・やす-める
	学校（がっ・こう）を休（やす）む to be absent from school　休日（きゅう・じつ）holiday, a day off		
休 休 休			

Reading Exercises

Write the readings. ♪Audio File 7-2

(1)	(2)	(3)	(4)	(5)	(6)
本 book	学校 school	学生 student	先生 teacher	日本語 Japanese language	名字 family name
(7)	(8)	(9)	(10)	(11)	(12)
先月 last month	先週 last week	名前 name	学ぶ learn	休む take a rest	休日 day off

(13)

ノートに名前を書いてください。

Please write your name in a notebook.

(14)

毎日本を読みます。

I read books every day.

(15)

学校に学生が二十人います。

There are twenty students in a school.

Writing Exercises

Write the words and sentences using Kanji. ♪Audio File 7-3

(1) にほん Japan	(2) がっこう school	(3) がくせい student	(4) せんせい teacher	(5) みょうじ family name	(6) なまえ name
(7) せんしゅう last week	(8) せんげつ last month	(9) ほん book	(10) きゅうじつ day off	(11) にほんご Japanese language	

(12) きれいに じを かいてください。 Please write beautifully.
(13) きょう がっこうを やすみました。 I was absent from school today.
(14) にほんごの ほんを よみます。 I read Japanese language books.

8. City

町	city	車	car	電	electricity	寺	temple
門	gate	駅	station	港	port	国	country
行	go	来	come	帰	return		

Now we come to a city.

There are many exciting words!

Do you notice that the left side of 港 port has three short lines? These represent water. Most kanji characters related to water have this part. This kind of kanji part is called **radicals**.

Wow, I see. So do all radicals represent meaning?

Not really. Radicals have been used to classify Kanji characters. Some of them represent meanings, but others don't. It may be helpful to memorize only some radicals which represent meanings.

All right!

Some characters represent shapes. For example, Gate 門 was  .

It's easy to memorize.

Yes. Another example is 車, car. 車 was  . The shape is very similar to see a wheelbarrow from the top.

Fantastic! I love drawing.

Kanji Writing Practice

♪Audio File 8-1

	Meaning	On reading	Kun reading
町	city	チョウ	まち
	町（まち）city		
車	car	シャ	くるま
	車（くるま）car		
電	electricity	デン	
	電車（でん・しゃ）train		
寺	temple	ジ	てら
	寺（てら）temple		
門	gate	モン	かど
	門（もん）gate　校門（こう・もん）school gate		
駅	station	エキ	
	駅（えき）station		

	Meaning	On reading	Kun reading
港	port	コウ	みなと
	港（みなと）port		
港 港 港			
国	country	コク	くに
	国（くに）country		
国 国 国			
行	go	コウ・ギョウ・アン	い-く・ゆ-く・おこな-う
	町（まち）へ行（い）く to go to a city		
行 行 行			
来	come	ライ	く-る・きた-る・きた-す
	電車（でん・しゃ）で来（く）る to come by train　来年（らい・ねん）next year 来月（らい・げつ）next month　来週（らい・しゅう）next week		
来 来 来			
帰	return	キ	かえ-る・かえ-す
	国（くに）へ帰（かえ）る to return to my home country		
帰 帰 帰			

Reading Exercises

Write the readings. ♪Audio File 8-2

(1)	(2)	(3)	(4)	(5)	(6)
車 car	駅 station	寺 temple	港 port	国 country	町 city
(7)	(8)	(9)	(10)	(11)	(12)
門 gate	電車 train	来週 next week	来年 next year	来月 next month	帰る return

(13)
電車で学校へ行きます。 I go to school by train.
(14)
来年国へ帰ります。 Next year I will return to my country.
(15)
校門まで車で来てください。 Please come to the school gate by car.

Writing Exercises

Write the words and sentences using Kanji. ♪Audio File 8-3

(1) もん gate	(2) みなと port	(3) まち city	(4) くに country	(5) くるま car	(6) てら temple
(7) えき station	(8) いきます go	(9) かえります return	(10) きます come	(11) らいねん next year	(12) らいしゅう next week

(13) くるまで　えきへ　いきますか。 Will you go to the station by car?
(14) らいげつ　おてらへ　いきます。 I will go to a temple next month.
(15) いぬが　もんの　まえに　います。 There is a dog in front of a gate.

9. Shopping

百	hundred	千	thousand	万	ten thousand	円	Japanese yen
何	what	買	buy	物	thing	店	shop
高	high expensive	安	cheap	大	big	小	small

There are many characters which are useful for shopping.

百 means hundred, 千 means one thousand.

What is 万? Why is there a unique character for ten thousand?

Good question! In the Japanese language, we don't say "ten thousand" but "one 万（まん）."

We have one more unit.

Oh, I see.

For example, 12,450 yen is…

I know it! It's いちまん　にせん　よんひゃく　ごじゅうえん, in Kanji, 一万二千四百五十円. I'm a genius!

Well done! Fantastic.

Let me ask you some Kanji questions.

The character 高 means "expensive." Then, what does 高校（こうこう）mean?

高 means "high" and 校 means "school," so… does it mean "high school"?

Yes! Well done!

Another question. The character 大 means "big." Can you guess what 大人 means?

Uh, 大 is "big," and 人 is "people." So it means "big people"… Oh, I get it. "Adult"?

Well done! 大人（おとな）is "adult."

I'm smart!

Another example. 大 is "big," and 学 is "learn." 大学（だいがく） means "university."

The character 小 means "small," and 学校 means "school." The word 小学校（しょうがっこう） means "elementary school."

Wow! It's getting easier to guess the meaning of Kanji words!

The more you learn, the better you'll become!

By the way, we'll learn how to call "junior high school" later.

Kanji Writing Practice

♪Audio File 9-1

	Meaning	On reading	Kun reading
百	hundred	ヒャク	
	六百（ろっ・ぴゃく）six hundreds　百人（ひゃく・にん）hundred people		
百 百 百			
千	thousand	セン	ち
	八千（はっ・せん）eight thousands		
千 千 千			
万	ten thousand	マン・バン	
	一万（いち・まん）ten thousands		
万 万 万			
円	Japanese yen	エン	まる-い
	七百円（なな・ひゃく・えん）seven hundreds yen		
円 円 円			
何	what	カ	なに・なん
	これは何（なん）ですか。What is this?		
何 何 何			
買	buy	バイ	か-う
	車（くるま）を買（か）う to buy a car		
買 買 買			

	Meaning	On reading	Kun reading
物	thing	ブツ・モツ	もの
	買（か）い物（もの）shopping		
物物物			
店	shop	テン	みせ
	店（みせ） shop		
店店店			
高	high, expensive	コウ	たか-い・たか・たか-まる・たか-める
	高（たか）い expensive, high　高校（こう・こう）high school 高校生（こう・こう・せい）high school student		
高高高			
安	cheap	アン	やす-い
	安（やす）い cheap		
安安安			
大	big	ダイ・タイ	おお・おお-きい・おお-いに
	大（おお）きい big　大人（おとな）adults　大学（だい・がく）university 大学生（だい・がく・せい）university student		
大大大			
小	small	ショウ	ちい-さい・こ・お
	小（ちい）さい little. small　小学校（しょう・がっ・こう）elementary school 小学生（しょう・がく・せい）elementary school pupil		
小小小			

Reading Exercises

Write the readings. ♪Audio File 9-2

(1)	(2)	(3)	(4)	(5)	(6)
何 what	店 shop	高い expensive	小さい small	安い cheap	大きい big
(7)	(8)	(9)	(10)	(11)	(12)
買い物 shopping	大人 adult	一万円 10,000 yen	六百円 600 yen	八千円 8,000 yen	大学 university

(13)
午後買い物に行きます。 I will go shopping in the afternoon.
(14)
大学生が一人と高校生が二人います。 There are one university student and two high school students.
(15)
車を三百万円で買いました。 I bought a car for 3,000,000 yen.

Writing Exercises

Write the words and sentences using Kanji. ♪Audio File 9-3

(1) にひゃくにん two hundred people	(2) かいもの shopping	(3) こうこう high school	(4) やすい cheap	(5) しょうがっこう elementary school	(6) ごまんえん fifty thousand yen
(7) ちいさい small	(8) かう buy	(9) こうこうせい high school student	(10) たかい expensive	(11) しょうがくせい elementary school student	(12) おおきい big

(13) これは　なんですか。 What is this?
(14) たかいみせで　かいものを　しました。 I shopped at an expensive shop.
(15) さんぜん　ろっぴゃく　はちじゅうえんです。 It is 3,680 yen.

10. Adjectives

明	bright	暗	dark	新	new	古	old (for non-living things)
長	long	多	many, much	少	few	気	air
元	origin, source	好	like	白	white	黒	black

Wow, many Kanji characters for adjective words!

Does the character 明 "bright" combine the Sun and the Moon?

Yes! The Sun and the Moon are bright!

Then, why does the word 明日（あした） mean "tomorrow"? If "明 bright" and "日 day" are together, it's a "bright day," isn't it?

Good question!

The night is dark, and when the dawn is coming, what is happens?

It's getting brighter!

That's right! That's why "tomorrow" is 明日（あした）.

I also have a question. The Kanji 古 means "old." Can we say 古(ふる)い犬(いぬ) as an old dog?

No! 古(ふる)い is used for non-living things, such as a car, a clock, etc...

The character 古 is combined 十 (ten) and 口 (mouth), which means ten generations have handed down stories by word of mouth.

Wow! Kanji is really interesting!

It is, indeed!

Kanji Writing Practice

♪Audio File 10-1

	Meaning	On reading	Kun reading
明	bright	メイ・ミョウ	あ-かり・あか-るい・あか-るむ・あか-らむ・あき-らか・あ-ける・あ-く・あ-くる・あ-かす
	明（あか）るい bright　明日（あす）tomorrow		
明 明 明			
暗	dark	アン	くら-い
	暗（くら）い dark		
暗 暗 暗			
新	new	シン	あたら-しい・あら-た・にい
	新（あたら）しい new　新年（しん・ねん）New Year		
新 新 新			
古	old (for non-living things)	コ	ふる-い・ふる-す
	古（ふる）い old		
古 古 古			
長	long	チョウ	なが-い
	長（なが）い long		
長 長 長			

Kanji	Meaning	On reading	Kun reading
多	many, much	タ	おお-い
	人（ひと）が多（おお）い many people		
多 多 多			
少	few, little	ショウ	すく-ない・すこ-し
	人（ひと）が少（すく）ない few people　少（すこ）し a few, a little		
少 少 少			
気	air	キ・ケ	
	電気（でん・き）electricity, light		
気 気 気			
元	origin, source	ゲン・ガン	もと
	元気（げんき）cheerful, energetic		
元 元 元			
好	like	コウ	この-む・す-く
	好（す）きな物（もの）favorite things		
好 好 好			
白	white	ハク・ビャク	しろ・しら・しろ-い
	白（しろ）white (noun)　白（しろ）い white (adjective)		
白 白 白			

黒	black	コク	くろ・くろ-い
	黒（くろ）black (noun)　黒（くろ）い black (adjective)		
黒 黒 黒			

Reading Exercises

Write the readings. ♪Audio File 10-2

(1)	(2)	(3)	(4)	(5)	(6)
暗い dark	明るい bright	古い old	新しい new	長い long	多い many, much
(7)	(8)	(9)	(10)	(11)	(12)
少ない a little, a few	元気 healthy	白い white	黒い black	好き like	少し a little, a few

(13)

古い車が好きです。

I like an old car.

(14)

明日どこへ行きますか。

Where will you go tomorrow?

(15)

小学生は元気です。

Elementary school pupils are energetic.

Writing Exercises

Write the words and sentences using Kanji. ♪Audio File 10-3

(1) しろい white	(2) ふるい old	(3) くらい dark	(4) おおい many, much	(5) くろい black	(6) あたらしい new
(7) あかるい bright	(8) ながい long	(9) げんき energetic	(10) すこし a few, a little	(11) すき like	(12) しんねん New Year

(13) くらいですから、でんきを　つけてください。 Because it's dark, please turn on the light.
(14) かみが　ながいひとが　すきです。 I like a person who has long hair.
(15) あのくろい　ほんは　すこしたかいです。 That black book is a bit expensive.

11. Foods

米	rice	肉	meat	牛	cow, ox	魚	fish
貝	clam, shellfish	茶	tea	食	eat	飲	drink

Foods! I love eating!

牛 is a cow, but we've learned 午 as a horse. They look too similar.

How can I know the difference?

Good question!

An ox has horns. The character 牛 looks like having a horn.

A horse doesn't have a horn. The character 午 doesn't have any sticking out part, right?

I see! It's easy to remember!

The character 魚 looks like a fish.

It does! 魚 was  . You can see a whole fish.

By the way, The character 肉 was  . It represents a piece of meat with bones.

I love them!

The left side of the character 飲 (drink) looks like the character 食 (eat).

Well-spotted!

That part represents eating. The 欠 part suggests a person who opens their mouth.

“Eating with open mouth” means “drink,” 飲.

Kanji Writing Practice

♪Audio File 11-1

	Meaning	On reading	Kun reading
米	rice	ベイ・マイ	こめ
	お米（こめ）rice (raw)		
肉	meat	ニク	
	とり肉（にく） chicken		
牛	cow, ox	ギュウ	うし
	牛肉（ぎゅう・にく） beef		
魚	fish	ギョ	うお・さかな
	魚（さかな）fish		
貝	clam, shellfish		かい
	貝（かい）clam, shellfish		
茶	(green) tea	チャ・サ	
	お茶（ちゃ） tea		

	Meaning	On reading	Kun reading
食	eat	ショク・ジキ	く-う・く-らう・た-べる
	魚（さかな）を食（た）べる to eat fish　食（た）べ物（もの）food		
食 食 食			
飲	drink	イン	の-む
	お茶（ちゃ）を飲（の）む to drink tea　飲（の）み物（もの）drinks		
飲 飲 飲			

Reading Exercises

Write the readings. ♪Audio File 11-2

(1)	(2)	(3)	(4)	(5)	(6)
肉 meat	魚 fish	貝 clam, shellfish	お茶 tea	お米 rice	牛肉 beef
(7)	(8)	(9)			
食べる eat	飲む drink	とり肉 chicken			

(10)

牛肉は高いです。

Beef is expensive.

(11)

魚を食べますか。

Do you eat fish?

(12)

毎朝お茶を飲みます。

I drink green tea every morning.

Writing Exercises

Write the words and sentences using Kanji. ♪Audio File 11-3

(1) おちゃ tea	(2) さかな fish	(3) にく meat	(4) かい clam, shellfish	(5) おこめ rice	(6) たべもの food
(7) のみもの drink	(8) ぎゅうにく beef	(9) うし cow, ox			

(10) どんな　のみものが　すきですか。 What kind of drinks do you like?
(11) にくは　たべません。 I don't eat meat.
(12) まいあさ　なにを　たべますか。 What do you eat every morning?

12. Body

口	mouth	目	eye	耳	ear	手	hand
足	leg, foot	力	power	体	body		

These are the Kanji characters for body parts!

I can guess the character 口 is a mouth! It looks like a mouth.

Yes, it does. 口 was  .

目 looks similar to the character 日, but there are two horizontal lines.

Isn’t it confusing?

Indeed. The character 目 was initially like this  .

Wow, it looks like our eye! It was rotated and became the character 目.

Yes, that's right.

There are more interesting characters.

For example, 耳 ear was  . 手 hand was  .

Wow, interesting!

The character for the body is 体, isn't it?

It looks similar to the character 休 (rest).

The character 休 (rest) contains 人 (person) and 木 (tree) and represents a person who rests near a tree. If you understand the meaning, it may be easier to memorize.

The character 体 is actually a simplified character. In the old days, it was written as 體, which shows that bones, which character is 骨, are linked together.

Wow, so many strokes! I am glad that the character 体 has fewer strokes now.

Kanji Writing Practice

♪Audio File 12-1

	Meaning	On reading	Kun reading
口	mouth	コウ・ク	くち
	口（くち）mouth　出口（で・ぐち）exit　入（い）り口（ぐち）entrance		
目	eye	モク・ボク	め・ま
	目（め）eye		
耳	ear	ジ	みみ
	耳（みみ）ear		
手	hand	シュ	て・た
	手（て）hand		
足	leg, foot	ソク	あし・た-りる・た-す・た-る
	足（あし）leg, foot　一足（いっ・そく）のくつ a pair of shoes		
力	power	リョク・リキ	ちから
	力（ちから）po wer		

	Meaning	On reading	Kun reading
体	body	タイ・テイ	からだ
	体（からだ） body　体力（たい・りょく） physical strength		
体 体 体			

Reading Exercises

Write the readings. ♪Audio File 12-2

(1)	(2)	(3)	(4)	(5)	(6)
目 eye	耳 ear	足 leg	力 power	体 body	口 mouth
(7)	(8)				
出口 exit	入り口 entrance				

(9)

入り口はどこですか。

Where is the entrance?

(10)

トーマスさんは足が長いです。

Mr. Thomas has long legs.

(11)

手でパンを食べます。

I eat bread by hand.

Writing Exercises

Write the words and sentences using Kanji. ♪Audio File 12-3

(1) からだ body	(2) め eye	(3) ちから power	(4) みみ ear	(5) くち mouth	(6) て hand
(7) あし leg	(8) いりぐち entrance	(9) でぐち exit			

(10) くつを　さんそく　かいました。 I bought three pairs of shoes.
(11) はははめが　わるいです。 My mother has bad eyesight.
(12) あのねこは　みみが　しろいです。 That cat has white ears.

13. Verbs

見	look	聞	listen	言	say	話	speak, story
立	stand	入	enter	出	go out, get out	会	meet
社	organization						

Now we learn many characters for verb words!

I found body Kanji characters that are hiding! For example, 見 (look) has 目 (eye).

Well-spotted! 見 was  , which indicated 目 (eye) with the human body.

It’s really a big eye!

In the character 聞 (listen), the 門 part represents the reading, モン, and the 耳 part shows the meaning "listening." The reading モン is not commonly used nowadays for 聞 character, though.

And the characters 言 (say) and 話 (speak) contains ロ (mouth) as these actions are related to our mouth ロ, I suppose!

That's right! Well done!

The character 入 (enter) looks really similar to the character 人 (people).

How do we memorize them?

They look really similar, indeed! Japanese children also struggle with memorizing the difference between these kanji characters.

I recommend you memorize 人 (people) first; then, you can recognize the character 入 (enter).

The character 人 is used as a radical, a part of a kanji character, to show the meaning, "humans." For example, the character 休 (rest). The character 人 is rotated and becomes this radical.

It may help you to memorize the 人 character easily.

Kanji Writing Practice

♪Audio File 13-1

	Meaning	On reading	Kun reading
見	look, see, watch	ケン	み-る・み-える・み-せる
	見（み）る look, see, watch　見学（けんがく）する go on a field trip　見（み）せる show		
見 見 見			
聞	listen	ブン・モン	き-く・き-こえる
	聞（き）く listen, ask　新聞（しん・ぶん）newspaper		
聞 聞 聞			
言	say	ゲン・ゴン	い-う・こと
	「こんにちは」と言（い）う to say "Hello."		
言 言 言			
話	talk, story	ワ	はな-す・はなし
	話（はな）す talk　電話（でんわ） telephone　お話（はなし） story		
話 話 話			
立	stand	リツ・リュウ	た-つ・た-てる
	立（た）つ stand		
立 立 立			
入	enter	ニュウ	い-る・い-れる・はい-る
	入（はい）る enter		
入 入 入			

	Meaning	On reading	Kun reading
出	go out, get out	シュツ・スイ	で-る・だ-す
	出（で）る go out, get out		
出 出 出			
会	meet	カイ・エ	あ-う
	会（あ）う meet		
会 会 会			
社	organization	シャ	やしろ
	会社（かい・しゃ） company		
社 社 社			

Reading Exercises

Write the readings. ♪Audio File 13-2

(1)	(2)	(3)	(4)	(5)	(6)
見る see	言う say	立つ stand	出る go out	会う meet	聞く listen

(7)	(8)	(9)	(10)	(11)
話す talk	入る enter	会社 company	お話 story	電話 telephone

(12)
土曜日会社の人に会いました。 I met my colleague on Saturday.

(13)

毎朝新聞を読みますか。

Do you read a newspaper every morning?

(14)

今日父と電話で話しました。

Today I spoke with my father by phone.

Writing Exercises

Write the words and sentences using Kanji. ♪Audio File 13-3

(1) みせる show	(2) でんわ telephone	(3) いう say	(4) しんぶん newspaper	(5) けんがくする go on a field trip	(6) たつ stand
(7) はいる enter	(8) きく hear	(9) おはなし story	(10) でる go out	(11) かいしゃ company	(12) あう meet

(13) だいがくをでてから、かいしゃにはいりました。
After I graduated from university, I entered a company.

(14) えいごのほんを　みせてください。
Please show me an English book.

(15) せんげつ　しょうがっこうの　せんせいに　あいました。
Last month I met an elementary school teacher.

14. Directions

上	top, on, above	下	bottom, down, below	左	left	右	right
外	outside	中	middle, inside	東	East	西	West
南	South	北	North				

These are words showing directions.

Oh, 上 and 下 look very similar.

Yes! 上 was , and 下 was .

They show the concept of "above" and "below."

Wow, it's interesting. おもしろいです。

The characters 左 (left) and 右 (right) look very similar, too. It isn't easy to memorize them.

Also, their stroke order is not the same.

Well, yes. The first stroke of 右 (right) is a curved line from top to left.

The first stroke of 左 (left) is a horizontal line from left to right.

Wow! But why?

右 was originally written as . You can see the right hand in this old character, can’t you?

Write a right-hand part first and an arm second. In the current kanji shape, the right-hand part is the curved line, and the horizontal line is the arm part.

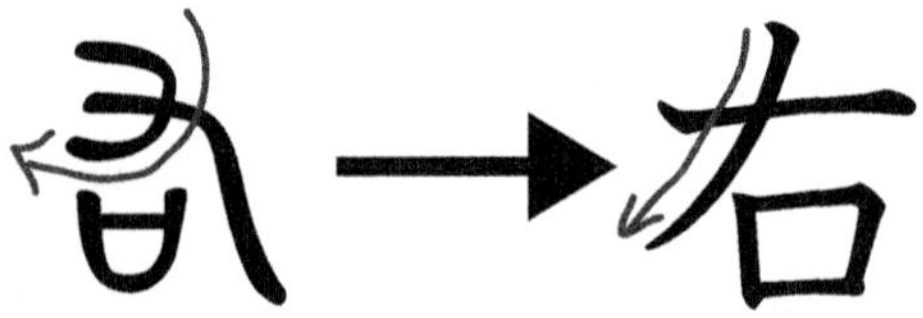

Yes, it is!

左 was  . Can you find the left hand?

Again, write a left-hand part first and an arm second.

In the 左 character, the left-hand part is shown as the horizontal line, and the arm part is the curved line from the top to the left.

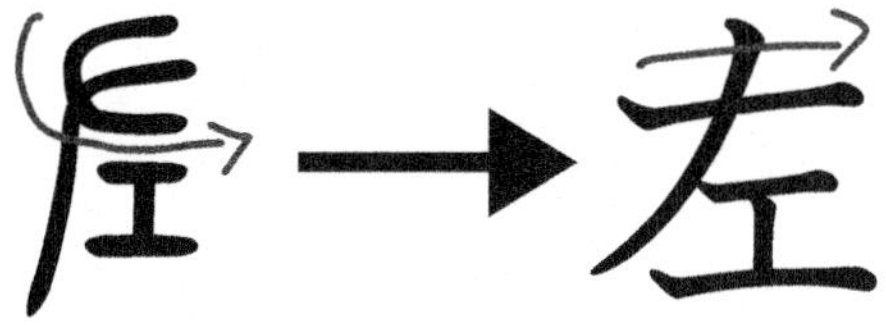

Interesting!

The character 中 means middle. Can you see a box skewered on a stick?

Junior high school is 中学校（ちゅうがっこう）, 中 means "middle" and 学校 means "school."

中学校 is literally middle school, between elementary school 小学校（しょうがっこう） and high school 高校（こうこう）！

Kanji Writing Practice

♪Audio File 14-1

	Meaning	On reading	Kun reading
上	top, on, above	ジョウ・ショウ	うえ・うわ・かみ・あ-げる・あ-がる・のぼ-る・のぼ-せる・のぼ-す
	上（うえ）top, on, above　上手（じょうず）be good at　上（あ）がる go up		
上 上 上			
下	bottom, down, below	カ・ゲ	した・しも・もと・さ-げる・さ-がる・くだ-る・くだ-す・くだ-さる・お-ろす・お-りる
	下（した）bottom, down, below　下手（へた）be bad at　下（お）りる go down		
下 下 下			
左	left	サ	ひだり
	左（ひだり）left　左手（ひだりて）left hand		
左 左 左			
右	right	ウ・ユウ	みぎ
	右（みぎ）right　右足（みぎあし）right leg		
右 右 右			
外	outside	ガイ・ゲ	そと・ほか・はず-す・はず-れる
	外（そと）outside　外国（がい・こく）foreign country		
外 外 外			

	Meaning	On reading	Kun reading
中	middle, inside	チュウ・ジュウ	なか
	中（なか）middle　中学校（ちゅう・がっ・こう）junior high school　中学生（ちゅう・がく・せい）junior high school student　中国（ちゅう・ごく）China		
中 中 中			
東	East	トウ	ひがし
	東（ひがし）East　東口（ひがし・ぐち）east exit		
東 東 東			
西	West	セイ・サイ	にし
	西（にし）West　西口（にし・ぐち）west exit		
西 西 西			
南	South	ナン	みなみ
	南（みなみ）South　南口（みなみ・ぐち）south exit		
南 南 南			
北	North	ホク	きた
	北（きた）North　北口（きた・ぐち）north exit		
北 北 北			

Reading Exercises

Write the readings. ♪Audio File 14-2

(1)	(2)	(3)	(4)	(5)	(6)
右 right	左 left	上 up	下 down	外 outside	中 inside, middle
(7)	(8)	(9)	(10)	(11)	(12)
上手 be good at	西 West	東 East	南 South	北 North	外国 foreign country

(13)
駅の東口で会いましょう。 Let's meet at the East exit of the station.
(14)
左手で字を書きます。 I write characters using my left hand.
(15)
あの中学生は中国語を話すことができます。 That junior high school student can speak the Chinese language.

Writing Exercises

Write the words and sentences using Kanji. ♪Audio File 14-3

(1) にしぐち West exit	(2) みなみぐち South exit	(3) ひがしぐち East exit	(4) きたぐち North exit	(5) みぎて right hand	(6) ひだりあし left leg
(7) じょうず be good at	(8) へた be bad at	(9) あがる go up	(10) がいこく foreign country	(11) おりる go down	(12) ちゅうごく China

(13) がいこくへ　いきたいです。 I want to go to foreign countries.
(14) あのちゅうがくせいの　おとうさんは　えいごが　じょうずです。 The father of that junior high school student is good at English.
(15) えきの　にしぐちから　でてください。 Please go through the West exit of the station.

15. Nature

林	woods	森	forest	竹	bamboo	虫	insect, bug
馬	horse	花	flower	音	sound	天	sky, heaven
空	sky, empty						

Here are the Kanji characters for Nature.

I found the Kanji character for horse, 馬. It really looks like a horse.

Indeed. In the old days, it was like  .

It looks cute! かわいいです！

The characters, 林, and 森, also look attractive. They use the character 木, which means tree, don’t they?

Yes! Two 木 characters became 林, woods, and three 木 became 森 forest.

Then, if four 木 are combined together, does it mean “jungle”? ハハハ

Uh…, no.

Two characters, 天 and 空, mean sky. How are they different?

Good question! The character 天 originally means head, as one horizontal line added on top of the character 人, person. It was written like this  .

Then, the meaning gradually changed to “something above human, ” such as “sky” or “heaven.”

For example, 天（あま）の川（がわ）, the river above us, means Milky Way.

Wow, おもしろいですね！

On the other hand, the character, 空, means “empty.” For example, the air is 空気（くうき）, 空 (empty) and 気 (air).

The sky is empty, so this character also represents the sky 空.

すごいです！

Kanji Writing Practice

♪Audio File 15-1

	Meaning	On reading	Kun reading
林	woods	リン	はやし
	林（はやし）woods		
林 林 林			
森	forest	シン	もり
	森（もり）forest		
森 森 森			
竹	bamboo	チク	たけ
	竹（たけ）bamboo　竹（たけ）の子（こ）bamboo shoot		
竹 竹 竹			
虫	insect, bug	チュウ	むし
	虫（むし）insect, bug		
虫 虫 虫			
馬	horse	バ	うま・ま
	馬（うま）horse		
馬 馬 馬			
花	flower	カ	はな
	花（はな）flower　生（い）け花（ばな）Japanese flower arrangement		
花 花 花			

	Meaning	On reading	Kun reading
音	sound	オン・イン	おと・ね
	音（おと）sound		
天	sky, heaven	テン	あめ・あま
	天気（てん・き）weather　天（あま）の川（がわ）Milky Way　天国（てん・ごく）heaven		
空	sky, empty	クウ	そら・あ-く・あ-ける・から
	空気（くう・き）air　空（そら）sky　空港（くう・こう）airport		

Reading Exercises

Write the readings. ♪Audio File 15-2

(1)	(2)	(3)	(4)	(5)	(6)
空 sky	林 woods	竹 bamboo	花 flower	虫 insect, bug	音 sound
(7)	**(8)**	**(9)**	**(10)**	**(11)**	**(12)**
森 forest	馬 horse	天気 weather	空港 airport	空気 air	花火 firework

(13)

先週電車で空港へ行きました。

Last week I went to the airport by train.

(14)
森は暗かったです。 The forest was dark.
(15)
山は空気がきれいです。 The mountains have clean air.

Writing Exercises

Write the words and sentences using Kanji. ♪Audio File 15-3

(1) もり forest	(2) はやし woods	(3) むし insect, bug	(4) おと sound	(5) うま horse	(6) たけ bamboo
(7) てんき weather	(8) くうこう airport	(9) あまのがわ Milky Way	(10) はな flower	(11) くうき air	(12) そら sky

(13) はなびを　みに　いきました。 I went to see fireworks.
(14) くうこうで　パスポートを　みせます。 I show a passport at an airport.
(15) あしたの　てんきは　あめです。 Tomorrow's weather is rainy.

Review Exercises

These exercises are similar to the Kanji test part in the Japanese Language Proficiency Test N5.

1. Choose appropriate Kanji characters from choices

1　ノートに　なまえを　かいてください。

1) 住所　　2) 名前　　3) 電話　　4) 日本語

2　りんごを　いつつ　ください。

1) 四つ　　2) 三つ　　3) 六つ　　4) 五つ

3　かようびに　おおさかへ　いきます。

1) 火曜日　　2) 月曜日　　3) 土曜日　　4) 水曜日

4　しごとは　ごじに　おわります。

1) 三時　　2) 七時　　3) 五時　　4) 八時

5　あそこに　やまが　あります。

1) 川　　2) 海　　3) 山　　4) 雨

6　ちちは　いま　いえに　いません。

1) 母　　2) 父　　3) 兄　　4) 姉

7　あのかたは　どなたですか。

1) あの方　　2) あの家　　3) あの車　　4) あの夕

8　ドアの　ひだりに　スイッチが　あります。

1) 右　　2) 左　　3) 上　　4) 下

9　らいしゅう　じかんが　ありますか。

1) 時間　　2) 漢字　　3) 学校　　4) 夕方

10 まいばん　ほんを　よみます。

1) 木　2) 本　3) 休　4) 体

11 こうえんに　いぬが　います。

1) 入　2) 犬　3) 大　4) 人

12 まいしゅう　とうきょうへ　いきます。

1) 毎日　2) 毎月　3) 毎週　4) 毎年

13 えきで　たなかさんに　あいました。

1) 店　2) 車　3) 駅　4) 会社

14 うみで　さかなを　つりました。

1) 魚　2) 馬　3) 犬　4) 牛

15 でんきを　つけてください。

1) 天気　2) 電気　3) 空気　4) 元気

16 としょかんで　のみものを　のまないでください。

1) 飲まない　2) 食べない　3) 書かない　4) 読まない

17 スーパーで　ぎゅうにくを　かいました。

1) 豚肉　2) 牛肉　3) 鶏肉　4) 午肉

18 いつ　おくにへ　かえりますか。

1) お国　2) お金　3) お本　4) お門

19 おととい　ともだちに　でんわを　しました。

1) 手だち　2) 兄だち　3) 夕だち　4) 友だち

2. Choose appropriate Hiragana reading from choices.

1　えきの　東口で　あいましょう。

1) にしぐち　2) ひがしぐち　3) きたぐち　4) みなみぐち

2　バスで　空港へ　いきます。

1) えき　2) がっこう　3) くうこう　4) びょういん

3　このくつは　一足　はっせんえんです。

1) ひとつ　2) いっこ　3) いっちゃく　4) いっそく

4　おおたさんは　ダンスが　上手です。

1) すき　2) へた　3) じょうず　4) かんたん

5　どうぞ　入ってください。

1) つかって　2) はいって　3) あらって　4) いって

6　あのおばあさんは　目が　あまり　よくないです。

1) みみ　2) くち　3) め　4) て

7　ほっかいどうで　黒い　うまを　みました。

1) くろい　2) しろい　3) たかい　4) うまい

8　さとうさんは　会社で　はたらいています。

1) びょういん　2) がっこう　3) じむしょ　4) かいしゃ

9　木曜日に　かいぎが　あります。

1) げつようび　2) どようび　3) きんようび　4) もくようび

10　へやに　男の人が　はちにん　います。

1) おとこのひと　2) おんなのひと　3) おとこのこ　4) おんなのこ

11　テーブルの　うえに　みかんが　九つ　あります。

1) ななつ　2) むっつ　3) やっつ　4) ここのつ

12　あしたの　天気は　はれです。

1) でんき　2) てんき　3) げんき　4) くうき

13　出口は　あちらです。

1) でぐち　2) きたぐち　3) いりぐち　4) にしぐち

14　がっこうの　前に　きっさてんが　あります。

1) うしろ　2) まえ　3) となり　4) みぎ

15　あした　車で　おおさかへ　いきます。

1) くるま　2) でんしゃ　3) ふね　4) ひこうき

16　月が　とても　きれいです。

1) そら　2) かわ　3) やま　4) つき

17　午前10じに　びょういんへ　いきます。

1) ひる　2) ごぜん　3) あさ　4) ごご

18　このくるまは　高いです。

1) しろい　2) くろい　3) やすい　4) たかい

19　小学生が　ふたり　います。

1) しょうがくせい　2) ちゅうがくせい　3) こうこうせい　4) がくせい

20　ぜんぶで　八百円です。

1) ごひゃくえん　2) ろっぴゃくえん　3) はっぴゃくえん　4) にひゃくえん

Congratulations!

You've finished all 140 Kanji characters and related words.

よくできました。Well done!

I hope you have enjoyed learning Kanji with this book.

Don't forget to download your Free Gift, the full Audio Tracks.

Go to the link below and download your Audio tracks.

www.funjapaneselearning.com

You can find the link for the download in the menu bar as "Bonus Download."

Select this book title and follow the instructions to get the audio.

It would be better to download the files directly to your computer, not your tablet or phone, and extract them there before adding them to your media library.

You can then put them on your tablet, phone, or any device you'd like to use.

If you have any questions, please get in touch with me at

asuka@funjapaneselearning.com

Follow me!

YouTube: Fun Japanese Learning

https://www.youtube.com/c/FunJapaneseLearning

Facebook: @Dr.AsukaTsuchiya

Instagram: @asuka.sensei

Answers

1. Kanji Basics

Reading Exercises

(1) かわ　(2) たんぼ　(3) ひ　(4) あめ

(5) はたけ　(6) いわ　(7) やま　(8) いし

(9) やまに　のぼります。

(10) せっけんで　あらいます。

(11) あめです。

Writing Exercises

(1) 田　(2) 石　(3) 火　(4) 川　(5) 畑　(6) 山

(7) 雨　(8) 岩

(9) 川の石は　まるいです。

(10) あそこに大きい岩があります。

(11) 山川さんが畑にいます。

2. Number

Reading Exercises

(1) に　(2) し・よん　(3) ろく

(4) きゅう・く　(5) いち　(6) はち

(7) さん　(8) じゅう　(9) ご

(10) しち・なな　(11) ふたつ　(12) いつつ

(13) やっつ　(14) よっつ　(15) ここのつ

(16) むっつ

(17) ハンバーガーを　みっつ　ください。

(18) テーブルのうえに　みかんが　ななつ　あります。

(19) たまごが　ひとつも　ありません。

Writing Exercises

(1) 一つ　(2) 四つ　(3) 三つ　(4) 十

(5) 六つ　(6) 九つ　(7) 七つ　(8) 四

(9) 二　(10) 十　(11) 五　(12) 三

(13) 八　(14) 六　(15) 一　(16) 七　(17) 九

(18) カレーライスを　二つください。

(19) けしゴムを　五つかいました。

(20) りんごが　八つあります。

3. Family

Reading Exercises

(1) はは　(2) ちち　(3) こども　(4) いぬ

(5) ともだち　(6) ひとり　(7) ふたり

(8) さんにん　(9) おとこのひと　(10) おんなのこ　(11) おかあさん　(12) おとうさん

(13) おかあさんと　こども

(14) おとこのこが　さんにんいます。

(15) おんなのひとが　ふたりと　いぬがいます。

Writing Exercises

(1) 男の子　(2) 女の子　(3) 父　(4) 母

(5) 友だち　(6) 子ども　(7) お父さん

(8) お母さん　(9) 女の人　(10) 一人

(11) 二人　(12) 三人

(13) クラスに男の子が二十人と　女の子が十六人います。

(14) 母と父は　げんきです。

(15) 友だちのうちに　犬がいます。

4. Days of the Week

Reading Exercises

(1) つち　(2) き　(3) つき　(4) おかね

(5) みず　(6) いちにち　(7) ついたち

(8) かようび　(9) もくようび　(10) げつようび　(11) きんようび　(12) にちようび

(13) すいようび　(14) どようび　(15) さんがつ　(16) ごかげつ

(17) にがつ　ここのかは　どようびです。

(18) にちようびに　はたらきます。

(19) アメリカに　じゅっかげつ　いました。

Writing Exercises

(1) 二日　(2) 四日　(3) 六日　(4) 八日

(5) 十日　(6) 四か月　(7) 火曜日

(8) 木曜日　(9) 日曜日　(10) 月曜日

(11) 水曜日　(12) 土曜日　(13) 金曜日

(14) 六月　(15) 十月　(16) 七月　(17) 月

(18) 水

(19) 四月十四日

(20) 八月に　オーストラリアへ　いきます。

(21) お金は　たいせつです。

5. Time 1

Reading Exercises

(1) はんぶん　(2) うしろ　(3) まえ

(4) ごぜん　(5) ごご　(6) じかん

(7) にじ　(8) よじはん　(9) さんぷん

(10) ごじ　(11) きゅうふん　(12) ななふん

(13) くじ　(14) しちじ　(15) よんふん

(15) じゅうにじ　(17) はやい

(18) ごぜんろくじに　おきました。

(19) ごごじゅういちじに　ねました。

(20) ぎんこうの　まえに　きっさてんがあります。

Writing Exercises

(1) 一時　(2) 二時　(3) 三時　(4) 四時

(5) 五時半　(6) 六時　(7) 七時　(8) 八時

(9) 九時　(10) 十時　(11) 十一時

(12) 十二時　(13) 二時半　(14) 六分

(15) 午前　(16) 午後　(17) 時間　(18) 早い

(19) レストランは午後五時からです。

(20) 時間がありません。

(21) 六時二十五分です。

6. Time 2

Reading Exercises

(1) ひる　(2) よる　(3) ゆうがた

(4) まいにち　(5) まいとし　(6) まいあさ

(7) けさ　(8) きょう　(9) こんしゅう

(10) こんげつ　(11) ことし

(12) いっしゅうかん

(13) けさ　あさごはんを　たべましたか。

(14) あのかたは　どなたですか。

(15) ゆうやけが　きれいでした。

Writing Exercises

(1) 五年　(2) 朝　(3) 昼　(4) 夕方　(5) 夜

(6) 今朝　(7) 今日　(8) あの方　(9) 毎年

(10) 今月　(11) 毎日　(12) 今年　(13) 毎月

(14) 今週　(15) 夕日　(16) 毎週　(17) 毎朝

(18) 一週間

(19) 三年前フランスに　いきました。

(20) 今朝コーヒーを　のみました。

(21) 十二時に　昼ごはんを　たべませんか。

7. School

Reading Exercises

(1) ほん　(2) がっこう　(3) がくせい

(4) せんせい　(5) にほんご　(6) みょうじ

(7) せんげつ　(8) せんしゅう　(9) なまえ

(10) まなぶ　(11) やすむ　(12) きゅうじつ

(13) ノートに　なまえを　かいてください。

(14) まいにち　ほんを　よみます。

(15) がっこうに　がくせいが　にじゅうにんいます。

Writing Exercises

(1) 日本　(2) 学校　(3) 学生　(4) 先生

(5) 名字　(6) 名前　(7) 先週　(8) 先月

(9) 本　(10) 休日　(11) 日本語

(12) きれいに　字を書いてください。

(13) 今日　学校を　休みました。

(14) 日本語の本を読みます。

8. City

Reading Exercises

(1) くるま　(2) えき　(3) てら　(4) みなと

(5) くに　(6) まち　(7) もん　(8) でんしゃ

(9) らいしゅう　(10) らいねん

(11) らいげつ　(12) かえる

(13) でんしゃで　がっこうへ　いきます。

(14) らいねん　くにへ　かえります。

(15) こうもんまで　くるまで　きてください。

Writing Exercises

(1) 門　(2) 港　(3) 町　(4) 国　(5) 車

(6) 寺　(7) 駅　(8) 行きます　(9) 帰ります

(10) 来ます　(11) 来年　(12) 来週

(13) 車で駅へ　行きますか。

(14) 来月お寺へ　行きます。

(15) 犬が　門の前に　います。

9. Shopping

Reading Exercises

(1) なに　(2) みせ　(3) たかい

(4) ちいさい　(5) やすい　(6) おおきい

(7) かいもの　(8) おとな　(9) いちまんえん

(10) ろっぴゃくえん　(11) はっせんえん

(12) だいがく

(13) ごご　かいものに　いきます。

(14) だいがくせいが　ひとりと　こうこうせいが　ふたり　います。

(15) くるまを　さんびゃくまんえんでかいました。

Writing Exercises

(1) 二百人　(2) 買い物　(3) 高校　(4) 安い

(5) 小学校　(6) 五万円　(7) 小さい

(8) 買う　(9) 高校生　(10) 高い

(11) 小学生　(12) 大きい

(13) これは何ですか。

(14) 高い店で買い物をしました。

(15) 三千六百八十円です。

10. Adjectives

Reading Exercises

(1) くらい　(2) あかるい　(3) ふるい

(4) あたらしい　(5) ながい　(6) おおい

(7) すくない　(8) げんき　(9) しろい

(10) くろい　(11) すき　(12) すこし

(13) ふるい　くるまが　すきです。

(14) あす　どこへ　いきますか。

(15) しょうがくせいは　げんきです。

Writing Exercises

(1) 白い　(2) 古い　(3) 暗い　(4) 多い

(5) 黒い　(6) 新しい　(7) 明るい

(8) 長い　(9) 元気　(10) 少し　(11) 好き

(12) 新年

(13) 暗いですから、電気をつけてください。

(14) かみが長い人が好きです。

(15) あの黒い本は　少し高いです。

11. Foods

Reading Exercises

(1) にく　(2) さかな　(3) かい　(4) おちゃ

(5) おこめ　(6) ぎゅうにく　(7) たべる

(8) のむ　(9) とりにく

(10) ぎゅうにくは　たかいです。

(11) さかなを　たべますか。

(12) まいあさ　おちゃを　のみます。

Writing Exercises

(1) お茶　(2) 魚　(3) 肉　(4) 貝　(5) お米

(6) 食べ物　(7) 飲み物　(8) 牛肉　(9) 牛

(10) どんな飲み物が好きですか。

(11) 肉は食べません。

(12) 毎朝何を食べますか。

12. Body

Reading Exercises

(1) め　(2) みみ　(3) あし　(4) ちから

(5) からだ　(6) くち　(7) でぐち

(8) いりぐち

(9) いりぐちは　どこですか。

(10) トーマスさんは　あしが　ながいです。

(11) てで　パンを　たべます。

Writing Exercises

(1) 体　(2) 目　(3) 力　(4) 耳　(5) 口　(6) 手

(7) 足　(8) 入り口　(9) 出口

(10) くつを　三足買いました。

(11) 母は目がわるいです。

(12) あのねこは　耳が　白いです。

13. Verbs

Reading Exercises

(1) みる　(2) いう　(3) たつ　(4) でる

(5) あう　(6) きく　(7) はなす　(8) はいる

(9) かいしゃ　(10) おはなし　(11) でんわ

(12) どようび　かいしゃのひとに　あいました。

(13) まいあさ　しんぶんを　よみますか。

(14) きょう　ちちと　でんわで　はなしました。

Writing Exercises

(1) 見せる　(2) 電話　(3) 言う　(4) 新聞

(5) 見学する　(6) 立つ　(7) 入る　(8) 聞く

(9) お話　(10) 出る　(11) 会社　(12) 会う

(13) 大学を出てから、会社に入りました。

(14) 英語の本を見せてください。

(15) 先月小学校の先生に会いました。

14. Directions

Reading Exercises

(1) みぎ　(2) ひだり　(3) うえ　(4) した

(5) そと　(6) なか　(7) じょうず　(8) にし

(9) ひがし　(10) みなみ　(11) きた

(12) がいこく

(13) えきの　ひがしぐちで　あいましょう。

(14) ひだりてで　じを　かきます。

(15) あのちゅうがくせいは　ちゅうごくごを　はなすことが　できます。

Writing Exercises

(1) 西口　(2) 南口　(3) 東口　(4) 北口

(5) 右手　(6) 左足　(7) 上手　(8) 下手

(9) 上がる　(10) 外国　(11) 下りる

(12) 中国

(13) 外国へ行きたいです。

(14) あの中学生のお父さんは　英語が上手です。

(15) 駅の西口から出てください。

15. Nature

Reading Exercises

(1) そら　(2) はやし　(3) たけ　(4) はな

(5) むし　(6) おと　(7) もり　(8) うま

(9) てんき　(10) くうこう　(11) くうき

(12) はなび

(13) せんしゅう　でんしゃで　くうこうへいきました。

(14) もりは　くらかったです。

(15) やまは　くうきが　きれいです。

Writing Exercises

(1) 森　(2) 林　(3) 虫　(4) 音　(5) 馬

(6) 竹　(7) 天気　(8) 空港　(9) 天の川

(10) 花　(11) 空気　(12) 空

(13) 花火を見に行きました。

(14) 空港でパスポートを見せます。

(15) 明日の天気は雨です。

Review Exercises

1. Choose appropriate Kanji characters from choices

1- 2) Please write your name in a notebook.
2- 4) Please give me five apples.
3- 1) I'll go to Osaka on Tuesday.
4- 3) My work finishes at 5:00.
5- 3) There is a mountain over there.
6- 2) My father is not at home now.
7- 1) Who is that person?
8- 2) There is a switch on the left of the door.
9- 1) Do you have time next week?
10- 2) I read a book every night.
11- 2) There is a dog in a park.

12- 3) I go to Tokyo every week.
13- 3) I met Ms. Tanaka at a station.
14- 1) I caught a fish in the sea.
15- 2) Please turn on the light.
16- 1) Please do not drink drinks in a library.
17- 2) I bought beef at a supermarket.
18- 1) When will you return to your country?
19- 4) I made a phone call to my friend the day before yesterday.

2. Choose appropriate Hiragana reading from choices
1-2) Let's meet at the East exit of the station.
2- 3) I'll go to the airport by bus.
3- 4) This pair of shoes is 8,000 yen.
4- 3) Mr. Oota is good at dancing.
5- 2) Please come in.
6- 3) That old lady has not-so-good eyesight.
7- 1) I saw a black horse in Hokkaido.
8- 4) Ms. Sato is working for a company.
9- 4) I have a meeting on Thursday.
10- 1) There are eight men in a room.
11- 4) There are nine mandarin oranges on the table.
12- 2) Tomorrow's weather is sunny.
13- 1) The exit is over there.
14- 2) There is a cafe in front of the school.
15- 1) I'll go to Osaka by a car tomorrow.
16- 4) The Moon is so beautiful.
17- 2) I'll go to a hospital at 10:00 am.
18- 4) This car is expensive.
19- 1) There are two elementary school pupils.
20- 3) It is 800 yen in total.

About the Author

Dr. Asuka Tsuchiya is an award-winning psychologist, qualified Japanese teacher, #1 best-selling author, and mother with two adorable little kids.

She majored in Linguistics and Literature at the University of Tokyo. She received her MA in Education at the Graduate School of Education at the University of Tokyo. During this period, she was also trained as a psychotherapist.

After working as a psychotherapist in the educational and medical fields, she studied human communications at the Graduate School of Humanities and Sciences at Nara Women's University. She received her Ph.D. in Psychology as well as the Best Postgraduate Student Award. Her Ph. D work was awarded the "Association of Japanese Clinical Psychology Encouragement Prize" from the Association of Japanese Clinical Psychology, Japan's most prominent psychological association.

Asuka sensei is now teaching Japanese in the UK, having qualified through the Japan Educational Exchanges and Services (JEES) organization, the most prestigious Japanese teaching authority in Japan. She provides high-quality Japanese teaching based on her profound knowledge of the Japanese language and education. And, as a professional psychologist and psychotherapist, she helps learners have more confidence in speaking Japanese.

Currently, she runs communicative and engaging Japanese lessons at multiple locations, including the University of Southampton. She's published Japanese language textbooks for students and teachers and got No.1 in various best-sellers rankings in Amazon US, UK, and Japan.

You may also love them!

Do you want to master Japanese Hiragana?

With this workbook, you can learn Hiragana and improve all four Japanese skills, writing, reading, listening, and speaking.

You can download all audio tracks of Hiragana letters and words as a bonus gift.

Buy it at Amazon: "**Complete Japanese Hiragana.**"

Want to learn practical travel Japanese sentences to prepare for your next Japan trip?

Get the New Step-by-Step Travel Japanese Program with two free gifts, Audio files, and e-Flash Cards.

Suppose you plan to visit Japan and learn practical Japanese, which works excellently to communicate with local people. In that case, the Japanese Language Learning Guide for Travelers is the best solution for you.

Check at Amazon: "**Japanese Language Learning Guide for Travelers**"

Are you searching for a perfect notebook to take notes for your Japanese lesson or self-study?

You can write English and Japanese together in this notebook. The Japanese squared paper side is fantastic for your Katakana writing practice. The lined side is excellent for jotting down information in English.

Three mini-tutorials are included so you can use Japanese-style squared paper confidently!

Check at Amazon:

"**Japanese Learning Practice Notebook** for Horizontal Writing Full Moon 日本語学習ノート 満月"

Printed in Great Britain
by Amazon

45160776R00064